T0316675

DARK LINES OF HISTORY

poems

Sithembele Isaac Xhegwana

Mwanaka Media and Publishing Pvt Ltd,
Chitungwiza Zimbabwe
*
Creativity, Wisdom and Beauty

i

Publisher: *Mmap*
Mwanaka Media and Publishing Pvt Ltd
24 Svosve Road, Zengeza 1
Chitungwiza Zimbabwe
mwanaka@yahoo.com
mwanaka13@gmail.com
https://www.mmapublishing.org
www.africanbookscollective.com/publishers/mwanaka-media-and-publishing
https://facebook.com/MwanakaMediaAndPublishing/

Distributed in and outside N. America by African Books Collective
orders@africanbookscollective.com
www.africanbookscollective.com

ISBN: 978-1-77931-492-5
EAN: 9781779314925

DISCLAIMER
All views expressed in this publication are those of the author and do not necessarily reflect the views of *Mmap*.

TABLE OF CONTENTS

INTRODUCTION NOTE

As clearly articulated in my recently published essay, 'Notes On An Aesthetic', "the promise of European education and the redemption promised by the Christian Bible laid its claims on me through disastrous, monstrous experiences"[1]. My journey with literature began at primary school as an orator. From 2000-2002, after finishing my honors degree in sociology, I was registered for a Master of Arts degree in Creative Writing at the University of Cape Town. This did not only mark a continuation of a creative process that was blocked by other academic engagement processes at the University of Cape Town and an acute Christian religious experience but also a beginning of an imagination around Indigenous Knowledge Systems that I had been actively running away from for over a decade.

It is approximately thirty years ago and my time to 'ascend the mountain' has finally come. My family is very nervous about the whole affair, as in the past few years the soon to be *umkhwetha* had courted other identities. As a young boy evangelist, I had clearly communicated my ideas of what I thought about the *amaXhosa* tradition of male circumcision. Manhood, the idea which this rite of passage encapsulated, could never be validated in this event - so I wanted to believe. As a born again Christian and a second year student in the University of Cape Town, I thought I had carved my *identity* elsewhere.

I hated tradition. My religious environment taught me to hate tradition; African customs. I was discouraged from understanding the dynamics behind whatever the African people whose culture

---

[1] English Academy Review, Volume 40, Issue 1 2023

(which was mine also) demanded as more than a way of life. I failed to understand the analogy of the ancestors and the consequent meaning that this symbolism has for those who are alive. I failed to see the meanings that the African people attach to their own spiritual world. So, even though I did end up being circumcised, I refused to partake in any sacrifice; or any form of activity that was tagged "ancestor worship" by my religious circle. I refused to eat the right shoulder of a goat, *umngcamlo*, that is part of going through the initiation rite.

I had decided to give my own spiritual energies to a foreign God I had embraced as part of my conversion to a new tradition; that of Christ and his followers. Just after my religious conversion I had also undergone another significant transition, securing a place of study at a historically white university - the University of Cape Town. These two incidents offered me valid reasons to aspire to a new identity, a perfect antithesis to what I was and surprisingly what (to my late discovery) I would always be.

Ironically, though, I started to become obsessed by my project of detesting tradition. As an unintended consequence, my own detestation of tradition started shifting away from that of the ancestor forms of worship that the African community (a clearly identifiable enemy, according to my religious inclinations) obviously offered. I started hating anything that smacked of any form of tradition, be it African religion or not. With the lack of a suitable word, I also started questioning Christian symbolism and worship. The academic environment also lost the appeal it initially bore for the intellectual novice that I was before I arrived at UCT for my first year of study. I started losing faith in everything that I had formerly attached value to.

At some point, I had to leave the born-again Christian church I belonged to as it could no longer accommodate the 'prophet' I was quickly becoming. In fact, after spending nearly a decade there, the pastor of summoned me to the cry room and said, "Brother Isaac, I think you should start your own church". This would be the beginning of a completely new journey for me, back to the African roots of my Eastern Cape childhood.

Instead of "starting my own church" I returned to the Methodist church where I had grown up. There I quickly progressed to the point of registering for studies to train as a minister. This was while I was working in Pretoria as a deputy director for Statistics South Africa. Before I could sit for my first exams, I could feel that 'cry room moment' approaching again. So, I prepared for it by summoning the elders and telling them of my new challenge – the calling from the ancestors to be a *sangoma*. They were very supportive. They relinquished me "to do what was right" with the proviso that once everything was settled I should come back 'home' again.

Instead, the road unwounded to unexpected possibilities. The cry room 'prophecy' was finally fulfilled as I ended up starting my own church after I shadowed within the African Independent faith healing church (of St John's Faith Mission that was founded by Christina Nku in 1906). The late Archbishop Fihla was my mentor. At the same time, within a lot of pain and doubt, I was also growing as a *sangoma* up to a point that I started practicing. I am a ventriloquist who uses both the Bible and oracle cards to dig into people's pasts, present and futures. For personal purposes, I also occasionally throw bones. I translate some of these 'rare moments' into poems that not only offer personal healing but also serve as media through which I transverse alternative worlds of thoughts. From the moment my debut novel, *The Faint-Hearted Man* appeared in 1991 up to date I have published extensively both in South Africa, Africa and abroad. Still, all these individual poems, articles and essays published in different anthologies are marked by one common thread: a creative engagement with my Xhosa heritage from both personal and historical perspectives. That is the platform that *Dark Lines Of History* utilizes, a creative ownership of both individual and collective *histories*.

HINTSA'S PORTRAIT

Through English picturesque, here
he stands. Overburdened with colonial
lexion, he still stands, an intransigent
opponent of colonial advance –
narrative of the war.

Possession of land through
nighnteenth century Romantic
imagination – ceded territory.

Here he stands, as a figure
of Xhosa Royality. That only
through political maneuvering,
Smith could be the true meaning
of a traitor.

Yet, this portrait cannot reflect
the realities of the many voices
still crying for a ceded throne,
Of which the climax was
the burning of Hintsa's kraal
and the mutilation of his body.

And even more, the exportation
of the king's head to the colonial
masters.

QUESTIONS OF IDENTITY

Below me, a picturesque
valley, dotted, with undulating
hills. This valley, wanting to nestle
on the hills that I, dumbfounded,
wish to confide in.

Deep in these hills, I,
having rounded other heights,
more abstract than the guilt-inducing
panorama below my feet, I sense
inabilities, far beyond those of sight,

in defining this scenery. I saw
them sink, these grass thatched
domes, these corrugated iron
roofs. Upon the swift impact of this
view, I seem to trudge to an even higher

peak. Alone, shivering, I struggle
to locate any pathfinders.
Having confided all, in the secrecy
of these desolate hills – trusting
that no one would ever hear

my dark secrets – I walk down
to face more of my humiliation:
in this place, that only a higher
force knows why, I have decided
to call home. No matter how

sharp the contradictions that this

vulnerability confronts me with,
it is now – and only now –
that I absorb, with an even
sharper precision,
that what has been, has been –

the past almost shuts out
in the present. And even more,
that perhaps my presence
here is for other things, other
than those that seem to lodge
their claims.

RITES OF PASSAGE

Why should you always leave
us, unannounced? By the river's
bank, we could not see the stone
sinking, the fort from where
you spoke with the spirits. Only

the brim of your hair sailed
above the river's face. Shining,
the spirit world fused with
the waters –

we would not deliver you. And now
the timeless drums wish to lure
you back. Even the pigeons,
flocking upon these acacias, they
plead, relinquish yourself from
the river people.

The vigil dance, *intlombe*,
seems to be the only meeting
ground. The offerings we have
brought, the transient song
we murmur, as you fluently sing –
all melt into the seamless tune
of your doom: half-human,
half-spirit.

Upon your return,
we do not wish to see you
divine the end of our courses
in life, and perhaps foretell

a new beginning –
along shores foreign
to our memory.

We are much happy to be
who we are and the tides
that billow-encroach
our enclosures in such
a merciless mode.

THE CAPTURED MAIDEN

By early sunrise this day
I should have long deserted this place.
The spaces far away
Together with my people
Have long forgotten the sight of me.
Early in the days of my womanhood
I left, in search of your kraal.

Many moons have I counted
The glimmering light consuming
Many by the weary banks of the river pool
Where, as first born of your kraal,
I have been master
Of your many ceremonies.

Legions
Long have they deserted you
Big piles of herbs their awards
Crowds behind them
Countless herds scattered
Throughout those sleeping valleys.

Patterning yourself after your predecessors
You suffocated me with your misplaced proverbs
The traditional conclave –
Your main residence
Has lost its relevance.

It is almost a hundred moons now
With me tendering your cattle

And me creating your music
Slouching with your medicinal bag
Over my tattered shoulders.

My defeated husband
Has long forgotten
The warmth of my now tired breasts.
I have to please your kindred
With all that I am.

The members of my clan
And those of my traded-in man
Have long been calling me
Through many dreams –
Gushing words from beyond.

With your baboon fly-whisk
And your chameleon head-gear
Have you shrugged their wishes
I could only own
Countless drums of my tears.

Today
I would like you to know
The contents of my last dream
Which I could not pour
Over your stone ears –
To leave you, unseen
For you would never release me.

Have I not paid enough
For the dream that brought me here?
Come, let us dance

For the last time now.

OSTRICH EGG CARRIER OF THE KALAHARI

Woman
Twenty ostrich eggs hang from your neck
Sinew net tied around your back
Holding you against yourself
Pressing you down.

The threads that run parallel
to your back
Patterned from dried-up leaves
From the African spear plant
Symbol of yoke and bondage
From your many life manifestations.

Like many children
Clinging to your back
Perforated ostrich eggs
Offs-springs of the hot Kalahari sands
Epicentre of eclipsed civilizations.

Twenty ostrich eggs
Full of reed-syphoned water
Vegetal twine plug sealing them off
Calabashes that you never drink from
Springs that never quench your thirst.

With their placentas dried up
Displaced embryos
That could never see their infancy
Still
Broken pieces pierced together.

Ornamental ostrich egg shell beads
Metamorphosing into dance rattles
Reserved for esoteric activities
Culminating into curative shaman songs
Tantalizing rain dances and trances

MAMLAMBO

Steeped into your deep
presence, the citadel
whose unity with the
morning light leaves
vestiges of your temple

in the abiding presence
of the river's eye.
Nzwakazi, leave me
be, while I compose
this song of rejection

dedicated to you, the
water muse. I would
not wish my sight
to let go of me as I
silently stand on

these slippery water
banks. In tandem with
the horrifying dance
of the wind-shaken
reeds, I whisper,

leave me be *most
beautiful girl*. I can
never climax into a
moment of intimacy
within your sharp

breasts. The symphony

11

of death, intertwined
within your ghostly
presence, is an over-
casting shadow over

 my own existence.
Holder of the rain
queen's stone, step
out from your magic
horse and reclaim

the other world
where your crystal
ball is intricately
hidden. The tragic
fables that you spit

through the river's
mouth could never
orchestrate a melody
of content for me.

STRUGGLES OF MEMORY

Unaccountable crimes qualify one to exile
To die away from family and homeland

Coming safe to mainland, to light my fires
Is all I prayed for

Could I have hoped for a garden of remembrance
Where the grass-weed grew fast and tall?

There could be no garden of remembrance
As tributes due to the dead,

were not awarded. As the white skulls,
un-mourned, still peeped their husks

From the rock-sharpened surfaces. There is
no garden of remembrance

As the insistent hands of degrading memories
have erased the nation's essence –

As the skulls of the unnamed, undignified,
Still hang from their bleeding necks,

as if to curse the Xhosa eclipse
When all those who dared, ventured,

through darkness, into the unknown.

There is no garden of remembrance

Where the mind exhausted
Has lost its tenacity

DEATH WISH

Tell them I am dead,
To all the wishes of the dead.

The stars, the moon, what more?
No longer matter in my world.

Tell them I am dead,
Stone-dead, beneath the red-dotted sky.

The drizzling, down-pouring of the rain
Struggles to touch my sand-coarsened lips.

The winds that stride can no longer move me
The waves, the storms can no longer shake me.

I am dead,
Like a stone, amidst blazing flames.

I am dead,
To the songs sung by the ghosts of yesterday.

I am dead,
To the clinker of the spears and the shadows of the shields.

The goat, the groaning bull,
Is no redemptive equivalent:

I am dead also,
To the trickery of the foreign gods.

I will not mourn the black beauty.

I will not detest the white legacy.

HOMECOMING

The wooden door is broken, the roof thatch
flags. The wind has fallen low. The clouds,
hiding behind our mountains, Amatolas,
seem deader than dead volcanoes.

And here I am – and here you are, mother,
Your dry hair burns in the winter sun.
Your face is pale today in its thin light.
Your hands, blistered, twist at your
chapped lips.

Yes, I am home again. But where is the cow
today, that would bellow as it calved?
And where is the horse that gallops as it
always did, from the crown of the hill?
There is only me, your son, who has come back.

Yes, you sent me away, into that other world.
It is ten years now; I have come home.
I kick the dust. My hands are empty.
My head spins, while you, silent,
bend to the fire.

Yes, you tried to bend me to your will.
You tried to make me one with the shades,
our ancestors. But, I feared those images;
I followed another light.
All you worshipped, I derided.
And still your silence is what I fear.
I kick the dust, unconsoled
by this old cooking spot, its ashes,

the charred, iron smell of the black pots.
Son and mother – we are back together

You, your cheeks as hollow now
as if you drank the wind,
And I, your child, whose stomach feels
horrified, knowing I am back at the beginning –

Here at home, where all guilt begins.

THE RETURN

Standing in the cold warmth of this sunset,
Hearing the primitive music of those birds again,
I see a world that stands only in its ashes:
Only some memories, of childhood, remain.

A place, encircled by low hills,
With its apparently fat cows and empty
green fields,
With the extravagant beauty of its mimosas –
This world is no longer mine.

Now, pop songs replace folklore.
History has supplanted legend.
Railway-lines have cut their tracks
through the ancient forests and goat paths.

A frontier once – a frontier still –
Blamed to Nongqawuse
Where we were 'maneuvered'
to enact a blood scourge
on a peasant kingdom.

War of the Axe, War of Mlanjeni,
Warm of Nxele, War of Thuthula –
Here, at the heart of this old unrest,
This bloodshed,

I stand again, like one of those
First peoples who, the waters
of the Fish, the Bushman's having failed,
Now must hunt amidst dry stone.

GENESIS

Once there was an epoch when
women. Men, paced around, searching
the river, the seed, the stone-fire.
They ate the rich sap that lives
in the intestines of the roots.

Once upon a time, our fires burned
tall, their flames opening the darkness –
as we chanted. Dancing, we unveiled
the reservoirs of our light.

There, our feet tattooing, we chased
the moon. We chased the blue buck,
the eland. We raced with the Bushmen
and the Khoi – even as far as the red
pillars of the stormy skylines.

We watched our high priests, sangomas,
negotiating with clouds.
They called roots by name.
They traced and chased death
back to its black caves.

But, while we were busy
with our dancing, our vigil, our beer party,
a great serpent came, from out of the North.
He whisked his red tongue,
our village turned into ashes.
And still the poet sings, still
I make these verses, years later,

Even here, where no cowhide drum sounds,
so we may find that river, those footpaths.
So we might find again the seed, stone-fire.

DAYBREAK

This road, gravel rusted, coiling back upon itself,
takes me to a dam that splinters in the light once more.
Early morning: there is a hint of mountain light, of snow
about this water's shine. The small shrubs, yellow –
budded, warn of spring. But is all silent.

These hills, surrounding here, have survived
many adversities, going back to Dias,
centuries back, to Nongqawuse,
her prophecy, our disaster. But nature,
summer, winter, has her own resilience.

All around me, still, there sounds the history
that almost swallows me – the testimony of men,
of women, children – all swallowed by the earth,
its darkness, their bones now rattling under
unattended graves.

But today, to me, these myths, that history,
Seem exhausted. Complacent, we are always
blaming them, Dias and his cross, Nongqawuse,
her prophecy. Now, only a tortoise, nerves
frightened by my footfall, turns back to

the water, that door to the river,
the shimmer where sun first strikes
its surface. I walk alone this morning,
without ancestors, a river that cannot
be tamed by any bridge, I can see
the forked fingers of the sunrise
straightening towards me – a reed that,

knocked flat by many storms, raises
itself slowly on this bank to seek
a single sheath of light.

PRAYER

Eternal Spirit, lift us higher that the trees,
Make us see the fires beneath the earth.
Make us walk more slowly than our fleeting breath.
Plant us in your passages
Beyond sacrificial blood and wooden temples.

May we not be proud of the she-goats, the groaning bulls.
Make us see you walking with the river flowing,
Accompanying, as you used to do, the perished sun.
Make us believe that the mountain
Is also your child, and that the sea
Is the only sibling of the blue skies.

Eternal Spirit, help us assassinate the drought.
Even if death grows bigger than we are,
may we be in peace with Nongqawuse,
her mermaids. Help us, to make pain and love
our own. Instill in us your present,
your continuous knowledge

That you may cease to be that ghost
Whose existence pounds
The delicate floors of memory.

REFUSING TO WORSHIP

When darkness
had slipped down, the youth
would have to march out of
his wood and plastic hut
in the forest.

First in the entrance,
The wooden post whose two wide
stretched arms pointed at two
disputing roads, seemed to be

scrutinizing his poignant
moves. The youth absorbed,
moved by the interrogative
stance taken by the silent
post, on his refusal

to worship. Frozen, his eyes
fixed on the red skylines
above the kraal, the youth
refuses to worship.

Many years later,
confronted with the same
visions - fragments –
he is still much unable
to recognize just a single
gesture from those he regards
as just the silent
pristine and forgotten.

Much bruised, his fingers
cramped – still breathing
the African air – frantic,
he carries on with his
search.

MAINSTAY

An overnight mist – left-overs –
captured by the mountain, oozing
from its ridge-tightened lips,
seeking to move on. Pregnant clouds
summersaulting, a mimosa terrain

with its thorn scrub huddling
beneath gum trees. Plastic
huts protrude from a dense forest,
an asylum for circumcision school
candidates. Only if the landscape

could be true to such stories;
a blood-thirsty tradition that
always refuses to account for
its botched circumcisions.

Pricking bush, stone white –
very white – like Ezekiel's valley,
nerve-wrecking heights, hill
snoozing upon shoulder of higher
hill, shadows caught in limbo,
a mist crouching over –
climbing to the summit.

Swallows, citizens of many
worlds now swarm this frantic
landscape. My moods swing,
with the clouds, as they rise
and fall upon unknown village
and city, tumbling upon

foreign cultures. But, here
is my mainstay, here in
this land where the sound
of poetry struggles
to be.

The landscape, having given
birth to many children –
like bastard offspring – seems
indifferent. After all, it
is in this landscape only
that one can trust, having
survived us all. Still,
when our stories desert us,
she is the one that embraces
them, and even us.

NAMING YOUR LOSS

You have spent well beyond a decade
suckling from the breasts of foreign lands,
and its people have put you on your lap
Of other languages that are confronted
by the flat consonants of the vernacular
you are found weeping. Imagine, a native,
upon return having to guess what you
once looked like. And the girls and boys,

former playmates, frown at the sight of such
a hopeless picture. The women's sighs, the
weeping of the rain and all about this place
that once absorbed you, like a spouse
entangled to a love-fearing partner, roll
backwards with every footstep you take –
towards the interior. Being not so dull,
imagine, discovering how useless you are

here, where belonging and continuity
seem to be commodities. Now tired –
understandably, the landscape has
been altered and young generations
have taken over – the mind seeks
refuge but left to wander on the
delicate borders of the wind.
Wretched, you retreat back

to those other places where
you had always known that you
never belonged, only that proving
others wrong was all you sought.

Your dilemma is that of a wounded
bird, upon discovering the blight
around its nestling ground. Name
your loss:
this is your only possession.

THE VILLAGE CARNIVAL

The village carnival, dancers
move their sinuous thighs as they
advance from hill to hill. I call
it such, these disenfranchised
celebrations with pain,

a phantom of the past. I used
to know it as such, when far
away we could hear its music
and run for safety in the company
of its offerings. A marathon,

we recklessly threw ourselves
in the mercies of its swing,
till one clear morning – if we
were lucky – we would be aware
that some higher force had
cheated us. I am

addressing you in the past
tense for such reasons:
that perhaps the magic never
did exist. Even if I can not

really work it out;
something has happened
and the village carnival still
shouts as it did when,
undefiled, I could still answer.

MEDITATING

I have thought so much
about another boy who used to pass
through here. With tender sunrays
still struggling to split out,
he used to define each activity –
only through what his forebears
dictated.

He used to wake up
pregnant with dreams of the land's
plenty. When his poems could
only be sung – he did not give them
such name then – to the beasts
that defined such a life, the summer's
sequel used to scatter him and feed him –
spoils of the African landscape.
Paralyzed by the gleam of the
corn's beard, he would hardly
think of the blood and tears
that have gone down.

And now
I wonder if perhaps this same
boy has moved on to another
village, on a higher ground than
ours. As I am struggling
to recover from the blow of his
persuasions, I wonder still,
why is it that world
only strikes me as a life
modelled only after death?

A REMINDER

think of me
when the country
and the city seem
to be pointing
fingers at each other
as if they were servants
serving different masters.

It was my theme.

think of me
when these two great
forces that work behind
the scenes of our lives
lay their bruising
claims on the object:
an image, of my poetry.

When they bang and hit
the mystery object; my
image helplessly caught
in between beyond any
point of recognition.

It is still my theme.

think of me
when the country hobbles
around to greet the city.

I would never say such.

the dreams of the
blazing flames projected
towards the city trouble
my mind, the hope of a
damned hell posthumously
awarded to the 'troubled'
village is a big joke.

This would never be my dream.

think of me
when two simple humans
struggle to hear each other.

I persist,
It is my theme:

when the country and
the city fail to recognize
the earth which will
always be the common
factor.

AT THE END OF THE JOURNEY

Will I lift up my hands
And scatter the shrilling bones
that lured me
The word of the stinking cowhide
drum
The gulping of the dead legions?

I sought to be a cannibal
I built walls, I set bridges
I wanted to see myself –
Reflected
In the gleam of the dead tree
And the satiric movement
of the water.

My chants were only sung
To raise myself above disorders
That only issues of predisposition
Could lay claim on.

Now, my demons play tricks
On my mind
The dead heroes I incited –
Theirs was a glory
never mine
An honour long sunk
In the dark sands of history.

Wind-whipped, I have to turn
my head backwards
The journey has ended

There are no more miles
to cover.

The fingers of my mind
will have to curl inwards
I will have to be content
that in the dark secrets
of history,
my mind has no share.

TO STEPHEN WATSON

Wordsmith of particular note,
you departed without letting
me know. As your last born
I thought I would be the first
one to know, still I would have
slid through the coast,
to your Citadel and brought
you aloe branches. Sleep tight,
send me a greeting to Homer.
Poet Laureate, you departed
before your craft could bloom.

Keep on, scribble your words
on that granite stone.
I will scatter your ashes
on your love nest –
the scary light of the
Cedarbergs.

SCATTERED FEATHERS

The only evidence of your departed
presence is this august presence,
the scattered feathers. Seemingly,
you have gone on to join the train
of those departed before you who
have gone missing; and still upon
putting my magnifying glasses on
these left overs – reaching out my
fingers to be able to own your absence,
yes, you are indeed an ancestor now,
my true saint. My dear, you are gone
now, as a true martyr of this cause –
how could I – in the haunting presence
these scattered feathers ever
commit the mistake of pointing
my fingers backwards?

LAND OF THORNS

Giving up on my escapades
Not only my hands and feet bruised
A breath that I can no longer hold
Dragging behind, all the offspring
       I could never inherit.

Walking away, I could never imagine
That carefully sandwiched between
       many memories
Could only linger baskets of amnesia.

Beneath your laps still lie
The whistle of the winds that can only
drive me back to the lure
       of the land of thorns.

When all I have been chasing has just
       been one moment ahead of
Every footstep I could ever take.

With every drop of water falling down
Beneath these strange mountains
A line of tear attributed to my fears
Has fallen down, I have lost count of
       the moments.

Like a defeated child
Coming back to embrace a consumed
       embryo
Mine could only be a journey in circles.
Never to reach a destination point

And never to own a defined territory.

IN THE MEMORY OF MAKHANDA

Now that you have left, and two centuries
Have sought refuge in the mystery
Of the many cascading moons,
If given a chance I could not even
Pick you out from a crowd.

Who am I?
But a little worm
Baked beneath the misty NtabakaNdodas
The Amalindas, a battle-fort
For the many regiments after you
In defence of the land, the old curse
That has driven many to war
Are a pebble-throw away from where
The many creased hands
Have pushed the dry *phutu*
Into my mouth.

Growing up, toiling the land
Of my predecessors
With these mountain slopes
Shadowing me
From the many pains I bore
And the many rainfalls
That were imprinted
On my existence
I never could have known
That many centuries ago a giant
Was raised by the Khoisan-queen
And a mystic-priest conversed

With the mountain-god.

I hear that one day at the prime
Of your magic days
Ordered by the great queen
You decided to desert
All the comfort you knew
In the mountains.

I say so, for you were the self-made
King of the forests
And the magician who resided
In the caves
The creator of Tai.

You marched down, and embraced
The pains of your people.
Not only that, you were
On the battle line
And never feared,
And never moved.

Why have they erected
sanctuaries
And monuments on our land?
As if we willingly handed
The land to us
As a peace offering.
After all that, it was not enough
Blood, bones, betrayal.

Colonial harbinger, only if I could
Have a lasting view

Of those crumbled palaces you
sought to defend
And the gothic kings who sat
On the sunk ivory thrones.

My lines are only fed by cries
From a forced out generation
Two centuries after your calculated
Dismissal.

Great carrier of spear,
 I need to let go
Of your blood-tainted rag
 I found scattered
 On these ghostly Gompo beaches
 As King Mgolombane is summoning me
To the old citadel on the hills
Of the long-winding Amatola Mountain ranges.
 The python whose feet are
 The roaring waves of the Indian Ocean
 And whose pillows are hidden
 In the caves, below the feet
Of Table Mountain.

 In my sleep, King Mgolombane
 Has shown me
 Sacred herbs to dig, revered
 Animal skins to collect
 For the festivities of the great king
 Are looming
 And the lure of the virgin dance
 Has re-possessed me.

MY FATHER'S SPEAR

In search of my father's line
of lineage, unravelled - with
such dexterity - indelible clues
are carefully packed on
the path of chaotic discovery.

A non-existent kraal, a long
sunk mud rondavel whose
 stick-bricks have long returned
to their primitive existence.
The bee-hive roof, imagined

only as testimony of primitive
residence, long swallowed
by the hungry rocks carrying only
green moss robed mud-dew.
This land of Spirit, the Place

of Thorns, so was it named by
those ancient warriors driven
away by a primitive version of
colonial rebut, is nowhere
to be found. Its people, too,

quintessentially from land and
place, whose footsteps have been
swallowed by the quick sands
accumulative in their fronts,
whose descendants only have

inherited a movement of loss –

identity and throne. Their precedents,
as they negotiated with the loss
of existence, deserted their
benevolent spirits baptized

assegais and spears, leaving
the long collection of bullock
horns scattered about - fleeing
from many regiments who only
saw through the eye of the sword,

now exiled in rocky places and
mountainous slopes invite me
to carry their fallen spears on my
shoulders and claim the scattered
bullock horns. In this unending

search for land and precedent,
the only visible remnant is a spear-
like rod that visits me only at night,
hanging from two poignant poles.
I wish to hold it, but no one could

perform such an act, its last custodian —
like my father - had left with no
trace of existence. The incense,
the only negotiating ground
with the departed spirits,

tendering me to the sword,
that is my preferred verb, until
one day I chose to hold it, out
of desperation, once again that

line of lineage having deserted me,

and there I was, seeking to retrace
their non-existent footsteps. In my
own ways, I had to retrieve my father's
haunting spear, a gateway to an already
 forgotten way of life, from my own

personalized vistas of dream-carved
memories, and pronounce once again,
that I was seeking to be a man after
the long line of lineage which made
my father the man who I was supposed
to be, a prototype of a man I hardly knew.

A LETTER TO THUTHULA

Whe Thuthula!, I have come to your place of worship,
our little *sivivana*, named after you. Carved deep in our
individual memories, is your imaginary statue, you
Cleopatra of our pastoral land. You should be there
girl, amongst those thorn-crowned bushes,
just above the now dry and filthy Xhukwana
stream.

In my hand are beautiful beads weaved
with my very hands, from our colors,
to continue building your crown that
enchanted those two men hungry
for love. This is the only thing I have,
enchanting queen of our land. I should
have slaughtered a white cow,

calabashes drowned in white foam
should be dominating this place with
their sorghum-smell. I do not own a
crystal-glowing beaker, where I could
shake *ubulawu*, to invoke your presence,
as the only transit to your imaginary

palace, far beyond those tall *Mhlontlo*
trees, in a land far far away, where the
stoic Qamata forever rules.

 Madlamini, whose services could even
bring those stubborn chiefs and kings
to my presence, right now, demands
a cow, which for me is another luxury

my father's house alone could never

afford, for such a service should be
accorded by women from all walks
of our broken kingdom. I am here now,
to address you as a caring mother,
for the troubles are too many.

Whe ntombi I still find it hard to comprehend,
how on earth did you ever do it? *Girl power girl,
girl power.* The famous love triangle, that
brought out sharp spears from the royal
house, is still a defining epitome.

And still, after you waged the war
of the Xhosa monarchies, they ate right from
your hand, here in our pastoral land all
the girls are queuing up for the slaughtering
machine of the present day imported
monarchy.

And still, one last question, was it you
first or Nongqawuse? Whoever could
be the predecessor, your *girl power* -
combined, still encircles our necks
with chains of slavery. Be a true Cleopatra,
 please turn the monarch's noses to the
other direction, towards our diminishing
pastoral land and our silent suffering.

THE MAIDEN RETURNS

Sleeping hills of my people
I awaken you
Only in the name of a dream that sent me
    away
I come, I come
Aware of the absence of my clan
I wish only to narrate my story
To these hills that remained faithful
    to your enduring presence
Earnestly have they sat here
For all these many moons of my absence
I can only burn my incense
As the essence of my home-coming
And shake my beaker
Captivated by its magical foam
As the only kernel of my father's kraal
As those I had to come back to
Have long left in my absence
My trade belongs and is owned by such
The benevolence that stands out
    the test of time, like
this enduring landscape
Perhaps
That was the only reason of my exile
To learn to master the art of communicating
With all the members of my clan
The living, the dead and the long forgotten.

VOICES FROM WITHIN

Hail you princess
Who could not rest in the wake of a dream
A foaming drum await you
Unseen by your naked eyes
A roaring bull greets you
Just above your tired hands
The robes you forsook
Running away from your strangler
Are being weaved by tireless hands.
As masters and dispatchers of your dream
We send to you love
In all its possible meanings
A beaker endowed with the magic
Of your own people
And those of your in-laws
Under whose influence you ran away
A tiger skin is ready
To cover your nakedness.
The eye of wisdom cannot see
Where human fault presides
We give to you what is yours.

PRAYER TO ULU (AFTER CHINUA ACHEBE'S ARROW OF GOD)

Inside my *obi*, I have laid an imaginary shrine
Ivory skulls of your great lineage of high priests
Dangle above my troubled fore-head
Great Ulu of the Igbo clan.

Long long long ago
When lizards were in ones and twos
Our forefathers carved you
King-god of our six kingdoms.

To you, we cry Great Ulu
The one who single-handedly saved us
From the tyranny of a vampire-god
In supplication to you, I break
    my last kola.

Being of the Sky's first weeping
Is our yam harvest going to be reduced
    to tinder?
Your high priest refuses to break
    these two kolas
A threshold to a new season of plenty.

Is it not your high priest?
Who chose to elope for two full moons?
With the mirage of the foreign gods?
Must we die, must we die of hunger?

Our medicine men's goat-skin bags
    have run out of camwood

The fire that flickers through the night
    vigil
Will never wake us from our bamboo
    beds
Great Ulu of the Igbo clan.

I can hear a solitary voice –
the tampering of the foreign gods
For how long must we delay
    our second burials?
And the melody accompanying
    the yam feast festivals
Retrace your footsteps,

From the journey to oblivion.

AT THE GATES OF XHOSALAND

At the gates of Xhosaland we have come, empty handed
we stand. From far away we come, with imaginary
landscapes as the only precursors of our path. Plenty,
glorious kingdoms and chieftaincies have we been
promised. At the gates of Xhosaland, the only thing

our bone fingers can lay their hold on are non-existent
graves, deep-dug on caves that are hidden from
anybody's sight, buried by the rushing of pastoral
armies from civilisations gone by. Imprints on the
sand-stones that desperately hold on crumbled
granite stone offer themselves as only a clue-

to the crumbled kingdoms of the original inhabitants
of this ghost land, not the Xhosaland originally
tendered to us. Red-pitched pillars from dust derived
ochre, only hanging from man carved memories.
Big-bellied men, self-appointed custodians of this
pristine land, now in ashes, only tender to us pieces
of history only to sabotage our thinking abilities.

Here we find no solace, only retreat back to the
trillions of years that claim our only existence.

We can only come back, only as ghosts that
haunt carefully packed archives – well crafted
non-truths themselves. Glittering museums
abounding the land only could crumble in
the face of our haunting questions, we reinvent

ourselves and carve new professions, digging

ugly truths hidden in this land. We still revisit those grave-caves with now abandoned kings and chiefs, on whose thrones now sit man and women whose blood has no lineage to them. We go back, with our heads banging on us, in fear of the most famous word – 'treason' and its equivalent 'prison'. We go back to assume our spirit-world existence, where no such fears exist.

WHEN I USED TO DREAM

The skies would push their blue covers
away. Spear-holding warriors would
descend the far-away hills and claim
their existence on my lowly kraal.
My grass mat would ascend the
misted Amatola's, with my spear
in my hand would I come. Sitting
below those grey-haired olive trees,
together we would converse, once
again burning with their fire would
I descend to the more reluctant pastoral
populace. Carrying that light, their light,
I would transverse through every hill.

But now, exiled from the populace,
supposedly speaking posthumously –
my claim is on nothing, as that
ancient wisdom only belongs to
those trillions of years gone by,
that only a candid eye of a sage
could transcend, only when I used
to dream.

THE HIDDEN MAIDEN

With our hopes high
We come to you chanting
Pregnant songs of undeclared love,
Naïve, we are defined
       through you.

Drunk with dreams
We run in the sacred ways
Deceived by visions, 'visions'
Echoing our emptiness.

You lure us into your secret nest
Only through our imagination
Deep in the waters we come
At the river's belly we stagger.

Clapping our hands
We retreat, empty handed
We offer our holy tributes
To the spirits who tendered us
       to you.

In the emptiness of daylight
We still sing, clap our hands
Hoping to still find you
Scattered in the abode
Of their persisting presence.

THE INITIATION MASTER

Through the sacred songs you sing
I hum my impending doom
With your almost perfect legs
    you dance
You dance, till only
    a god is seen striding.

Blind-folded I walk
Every step of the way behind
    your stupid dreams
I stagger,
I still think, you are
    the master.

Gleaner of my many dreams
    you mislead me
You tell me you masterminded
    every dream
I nod, yes master of none.

I dance, I dance
I stagger, it can only be my problem
You ran away long
Before you penned my fall.

Very late in the day
I come to realise
The dreams were mine
I am the master of my dreams.

EPITOME

I will serenade, music from afar
lyrics cascading like misty rains
that calm my breath –

Idyllic winds will carry me far, far
on the rocky sands I have imprinted
my footsteps on, above
frozen seas I view

a mystic panorama. I crouch
below lowly grounds
the Okavango caves enclave me
with their ancient tablets, aloud
I pronounce my new profession –

I foretell of the abode, of African
saints – priests and priestesses –
their garments carved in anger
hanging from beneath deep waters,

I see creatures, creatures possess
my inner being –
I wish I were a song I could sing
with the melody of yesterday.

For eternities I could serenade,
a bard bread out of the red
and desolate soils of Africa –
barefooted on itching grounds
of the ancient territories.

With a desolate voice, I
lay claim on songs from an
engagement bell, far from
beneath the waters –
closely knitted with my being.

MAKHANDA'S GRAVE:

I

Star-lobbed giant crabs, lion-headed,
emerge from deep caves of the blue
water canvass, their heads decorated

with spear-holding warriors, many
warriors. Suddenly, a marine figure
emerges, bowing its humiliated

head near the blue water
canvass of Cove Rock, Makana,
war doctor and philosopher,

pleading with the Xhosa gods
on the art of war, a long
barricade of English men

holding war machines,
pointing at Makana and his
pastoral congregants,

only waiting for the final
moment, when this trouble-
some strategist would give

up on his meditations, and
eventually descend the rocky
sands to surrender, abandoning

the hope, the only hope of
his congregants, who had

followed him all the way from

a land invaded by these
same people, 1819, just one
year older than the famous

1820 English Settlers movement,
Makana had been commander
of another war, after just abandoning

another profession, African priest
and missionary, creator of Tai,
an African version of the Euro-centric
Christ.

The same people, here gain,
after heeding to a pristine
call, gathered in a crowd

seated, like men and women
would do during one of
those sacred moments

in and around the kraal, before the
bellowing of a bull, that bellow
ushering in the arrival of this

nation's lion-spirit, the giant
of war. Here, Makana, had
promised that the lion-headed

spirit would emerge, right
from the belly of the blue

water canvass, only after

a big jump. Criss-crossed,
Makana would jump from
one end to another, holding

the hope of the nation in
his breast, the only hope.
Only, to be dragged to a far

away Island, infamous for
snatching fire brands like
him. Only because Makana

was Makana, he still promised
his congregants, that he would
still come back, a truly resurrected

brother of Tai, still carrying
the hope of the nation behind
him. Still, many of his congregants

followed him to the abandoned
island. There is no giving up.
There has never been such.

II
Centuries later, here I stand,
on these same shores, over-
looking the now ghostly Cove

Rock, a huge crowd behind
me, hitting African drums,

ululating, shaking the *ubulawu*
beaker to summon *ookhokho*,
the lion-headed spirit. I am here,
on a solo journey to claim the

heritage of those men and women
long buried beneath the canvass
of these blue waters, forests, rivers

and caves. Summoned by
the lion-headed spirit, here
I stand, with all my bones

shaking, waiting, for the
emerging of the emancipator,
right from the carpet

of this blue water canvass.
Hoping, by the mere glimpse
of these spirits, I would have

been baptized, into the long
lineage of those holding
Makana's magic bag, a

medicine man never happy
to hold one spear. The same
star-lobbed giant crabs

emerge, spear holding
warriors. In fear-like
desperation, I retreat

back, to the grass thatched
medicine hut, the only geographic
panorama that gives me

the sense of home and belonging.

SKY - MOUNTAINS

There are no mountains over there
only undefined territories, slopes,
unlimited by culture or nationality
master strokes lazily resting
on eastern canvasses.

Rooted above many waters,
 roaring waves that bark
the world around. I see them,
every morning, just before
the morning star cuts

the eastern horizons. Dark
clouds hanging, red pillars,
ornamental - like minstrel
doeks. These sky-mountains,

never move, albatrossed,
like paintings from masters
of ages gone by. Mirroring
the Amatholes, the Ukhahlambas
and the Sugar-loaves.

I see them, staring at me,
as if demanding strokes of my
almost dried up ink pad.

IF ONLY THOSE GRAVES COULD SPEAK

They would loudly tell the truth, of the heroic deeds
we did in the past, as those we performed such on
their behalf are now on denial, a complacent
generation, whose deeds are only determined
to erase our existence, not only the monuments,

still standing tall, on the pavements of their
acts of amnesia. How could they, in the midst
of the many testimonies from those shouting
monuments, standing tall, to defend us from
the vagabonds who only seek to erase us, and

even the trace of our descendants, from the
indelible pages of history? We did exist, and
our deeds out of love were performed. We
stand here, in full watch of what we fought
for, now in the hands of the many minorities

who, in their less understanding of our
sacrifices still shout out in denial of our
very existence. Only because their very
design and existence is only that of
squandor. Those graves will not only

speak but will sing, songs that will
lift us up from this dust of non-existence,
and together we will walk and claim the
existence that was ours. Like a true
diaspora here we sit, with no voice at all.
If only those graves could speak!

NOMTSHWEBELELE'S STONE

By the river's side it lays, deep in the
running waters it rears up its head,
its shining surface standing like
a throne for the spirits. Standing

on the bank of the riverside,
addressing the ancient spirits
it waves its hand towards me,
the crab watches over, laughing

at me. Back at my maternal
home, the ancient homestead,
this big stone was disturbed from
its sleep amongst my grandmother's

possessions that had long returned
to the earth's compost, maybe
her long pipe, maybe her beaded
necklaces and maybe the *isacholo*

she passed on to my grandfather
on the eve of their courting. This
huge stone, together with a rusted
coin from Mozambique, now lost,
 are the only prized possessions
I found on Nomtshwebelele's site,
the grandmother I never had
a privilege to see. This huge stone,

still sleeps silently next to the
rondavel I built at the same spot

where Nomtshwebelele's rondavel
sunk after a mysterious fire.

This must have been her
grinding stone, or maybe
a throne where she sat when
she communed with the long

dead spirits, while enhaling
her long pipe, if she had one,
and carefully counting her
ornamental beads carefully

scattered through her body.

MANCHESTER ARENA BLAST

Here rests his head upon the lap of earth
A youth to fortune and fame unknown.
Fair Science frowned not on his humble birth,
And Melancholy marked him for his own.
("Elegy Written In A Country Church Yard" – Thomas Gray)

In the stillness of the night, this day I caught
the light - four decades back. Sitting on my bed,
at the pinnacle of my village hut, the muse
releases her ancient kiss,

One has to take that burden,
for the Lady of Honor might pass you by
when next she nods her head, when singers
have to release their magic.

Funny enough, not a day designed for
 melancholies. I, having celebrated on its
eve with a thanksgiving, performed
in the confines of a church court yard,

I revisit ancient English masters,
and there I dig on their elegies.
The same night, in a city
 in another continent, as the

sirene weaves his magic, the curse
of the ancient king falls upon him,
ruthless Edward The First, so cried
the choir of poets who survived

the wretched spear. Eclipse
of humankind, assassination
of the star of hope; true epitaphs
of a third world war.

Mmap New African Poets Series

If you have enjoyed *Dark Lines of History*, consider these other fine books in the **New African Poets Series** from *Mwanaka Media and Publishing:*

I Threw a Star in a Wine Glass by Fethi Sassi
Best New African Poets 2017 Anthology by Tendai R Mwanaka and Daniel Da Purificacao
Logbook Written by a Drifter by Tendai Rinos Mwanaka
Mad Bob Republic: Bloodlines, Bile and a Crying Child by Tendai Rinos Mwanaka
Zimbolicious Poetry Vol 1 by Tendai R Mwanaka and Edward Dzonze
Zimbolicious Poetry Vol 2 by Tendai R Mwanaka and Edward Dzonze
Zimbolicious: An Anthology of Zimbabwean Literature and Arts, Vol 3 by Tendai Mwanaka
Under The Steel Yoke by Jabulani Mzinyathi
Fly in a Beehive by Thato Tshukudu
Bounding for Light by Richard Mbuthia
Sentiments by Jackson Matimba
Best New African Poets 2018 Anthology by Tendai R Mwanaka and Nsah Mala
Words That Matter by Gerry Sikazwe
The Ungendered by Delia Watterson
Ghetto Symphony by Mandla Mavolwane
Sky for a Foreign Bird by Fethi Sassi
A Portrait of Defiance by Tendai Rinos Mwanaka
Zimbolicious: An Anthology of Zimbabwean Literature and Arts, Vol 4 by Tendai Mwanaka and Jabulani Mzinyathi
When Escape Becomes the only Lover by Tendai R Mwanaka
ويَسۡ مَرُ الهَيۡلُ فِى ثِفَتَي...وَلِغَمَام by Fethi Sassi
A Letter to the President by Mbizo Chirasha

This is not a poem by Richard Inya
Pressed flowers by John Eppel
Righteous Indignation by Jabulani Mzinyathi:
Blooming Cactus by Mikateko Mbambo
Rhythm of Life by Olivia Ngozi Osouha
Travellers Gather Dust and Lust by Gabriel Awuah Mainoo
Chitungwiza Mushamukuru: An Anthology from Zimbabwe's Biggest Ghetto Town by Tendai Rinos Mwanaka
Zimbolicious: An Anthology of Zimbabwean Literature and Arts, Vol 5 by Tendai Mwanaka
Because Sadness is Beautiful? by Tanaka Chidora
Of Fresh Bloom and Smoke by Abigail George
Shades of Black by Edward Dzonze
Best New African Poets 2020 Anthology by Tendai Rinos Mwanaka, Lorna Telma Zita and Balddine Moussa
This Body is an Empty Vessel by Beaton Galafa
Between Places by Tendai Rinos Mwanaka
Best New African Poets 2021 Anthology by Tendai Rinos Mwanaka, Lorna Telma Zita and Balddine Moussa
Zimbolicious: An Anthology of Zimbabwean Literature and Arts, Vol 6 by Tendai Mwanaka and Chenjerai Mhondera
A Matter of Inclusion by Chad Norman
Keeping the Sun Secret by Mariel Awendit
ه‍ﺘﻠﺘُﺒﻨُﻮﺘﻜُﻟ ّﺟﺲ‍by Tendai Rinos Mwanaka
Ghetto Blues by Tendai Rinos Mwanaka
Zimbolicious: An Anthology of Zimbabwean Literature and Arts, Vol 7 by Tendai Rinos Mwanaka and Tanaka Chidora
Best New African Poets 2022 Anthology by Tendai Rinos Mwanaka and Helder Simbad

Soon to be released

a sky is falling by Nica Cornell
The politics of Life by Mandhla Mavolwane

https://facebook.com/MwanakaMediaAndPublishing/

Printed in the United States
by Baker & Taylor Publisher Services